From Conception to Birth:
My 38-Week Journey

As told by Caroline Eva

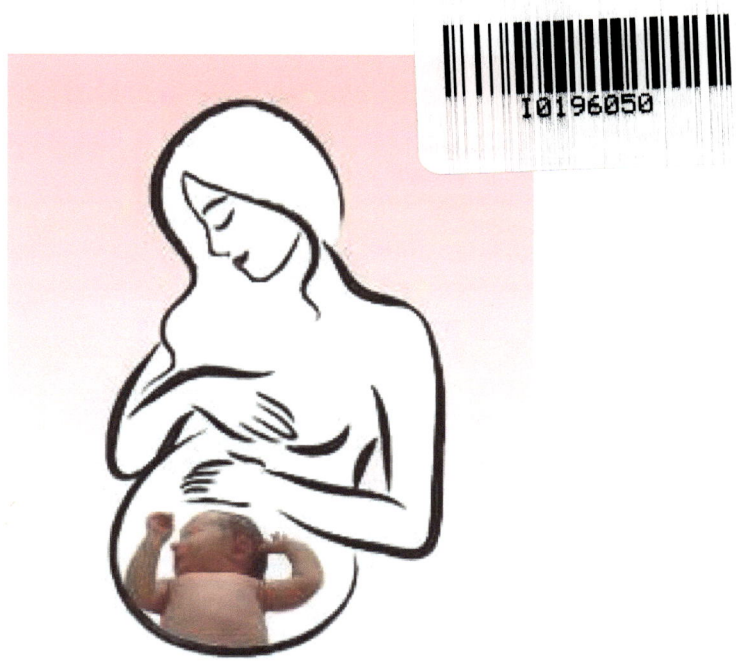

Ricardo Lewitus MD

Author of What Does The Sign Say?

Hello everybody, my name is Caroline Eva, and this is the story of my 38-week journey as a fetus. I have no way to confirm it, but this is how I believe my voyage started. For two weeks, my mother was preparing to have me. She was talking about the last day of her menstrual period, an egg, a spermatozoid, and suddenly a zygote consisting of 46 chromosomes.

CONTENTS

March 10, 2016 1
    Week 0 1
March 17, 2016 6
    Week 1 6
March 24, 2016 (Size: 0.118") 7
    Week 2 7
March 31, 2016 (Size: 0.13") 8
    Week 3 8
April 7, 2016 (Size: 0.25", weight negligible) 9
    Week 4 9
April 14, 2016 (Size: 0.4", weight still negligible) 10
    Week 5 10
April 21, 2016 (Size: 0.5", 0.04oz) 11
    Week 6 11
April 28, 2016 (Size: 0.9", 0.07oz) 12
    Week 7 12
May 5, 2016 (Size: 1.25", 0.14oz) 13
    Week 8 13
May 12, 2016 (Size: 1.61", 0.25oz) 14
    Week 9 14
May 19, 2016 (Size: 2.13", 0.49oz) 15
    Week 10 15
May 26, 2016 (Size: 2.9", 0.81oz) 16
    Week 11 16
June 2, 2016 (Size: 3.9", 1.5oz) 17
    Week 12 17
June 9, 2016 (Size: 4", 2.4oz) 18
    Week 13 18
June 16, 2016 (Size: 4.5", 3.5oz) 19

- Week 14 19
- June 23, 2016 (Size: 5.12", 4.94oz) 20
  - Week 15 20
- June 30, 2016 (Size: 5.5", 6.7oz) 21
  - Week 16 21
- July 7, 2016 (Size: 6", 8.4oz) 22
  - Week 17 22
- July 14, 2016 (Size: 10.5", 10oz) 23
  - Week 18 23
- July 21, 2016 (Size: 10.58", 12oz) 24
  - Week 19 24
- July 28, 2016 (Size: 11", 15oz) 25
  - Week 20 25
- August 4, 2016 (Size: 11.4", 1.1lbs) 26
  - Week 21 26
- August 11, 2016 (Size:12", 1.3lbs) 27
  - Week 22 27
- August 18, 2016 (Size: 13.6", 1.5lbs) 28
  - Week 23 28
- August 25, 2016 (Size: 14", 1.7lbs) 29
  - Week 24 29
- September 1, 2016 (Size: 14.4", 1.9lbs) 30
  - Week 25 30
- September 8, 2016 (My size: 15", 2.2lbs) 31
  - Week 26 31
- September 15, 2016 (Size:15.2", 2.5lbs) 32
  - Week 27 32
- September 22, 2016 (Size: 15.7", 2.91lbs) 33
  - Week 28 33
- September 29, 2016 (Size: 16.2", 3lbs) 34

Week 29 34
October 6, 2016 (Size: 16.7", 3.8lbs) 35
  Week 30 35
October 13, 2016 (Size: 17.2", 4.2lbs) 36
  Week 31 36
October 20, 2016 (Size: 17.7", 4.7lbs) 37
  Week 32 37
October 27, 2016 (Size: 18", 5.3lbs) 38
  Week 33 38
November 3, 2016 (Size: 18.6", 5.78lbs) 39
  Week 34 39
November 10, 2016 (Size: 19", 6.3lbs) 40
  Week 35 40
November 17, 2016 (Size: 19.5", 6.8lbs) 41
  Week 36 41
November 24, 2016 (Size: 20", 7lbs) 42
  Week 37 42
December 1, 2016 (Size: 10.2", 7.6lbs) 43
  Week 38 43
Disclaimers 45

March 10, 2016

Week 0

Day 1. My parents love each other so much that they decided to share their love and create sweet me, future Caroline Eva. I will call Day 1 a successful fertilization between my father's sperm and my mother's ovule.

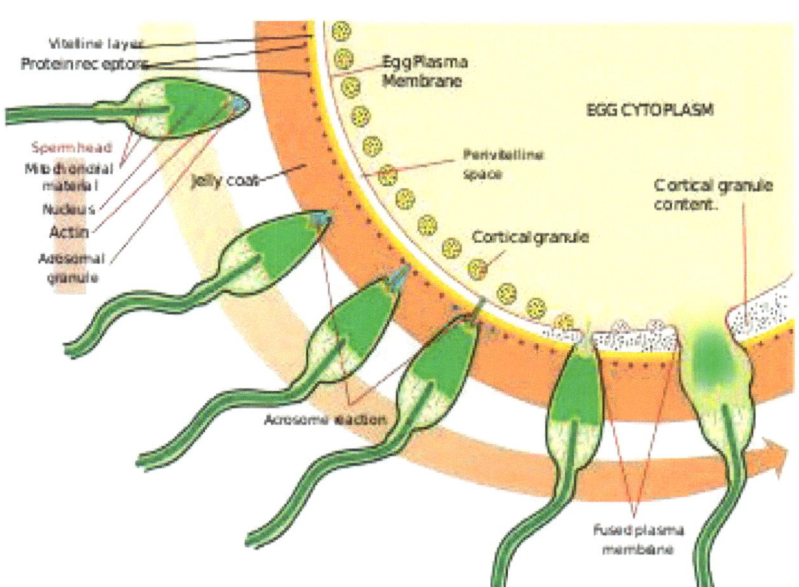

Acrosome reaction on a Sea Urchin cell

Who knew that sea urchins did it the same way? Ha!

Day 2. My genome is activated with around three billion DNA base pairs. This is very serious stuff. It is not about the birds and the bees; you can clearly visualize my sex chromosomes that came from my parents. I have double XX chromosomes.

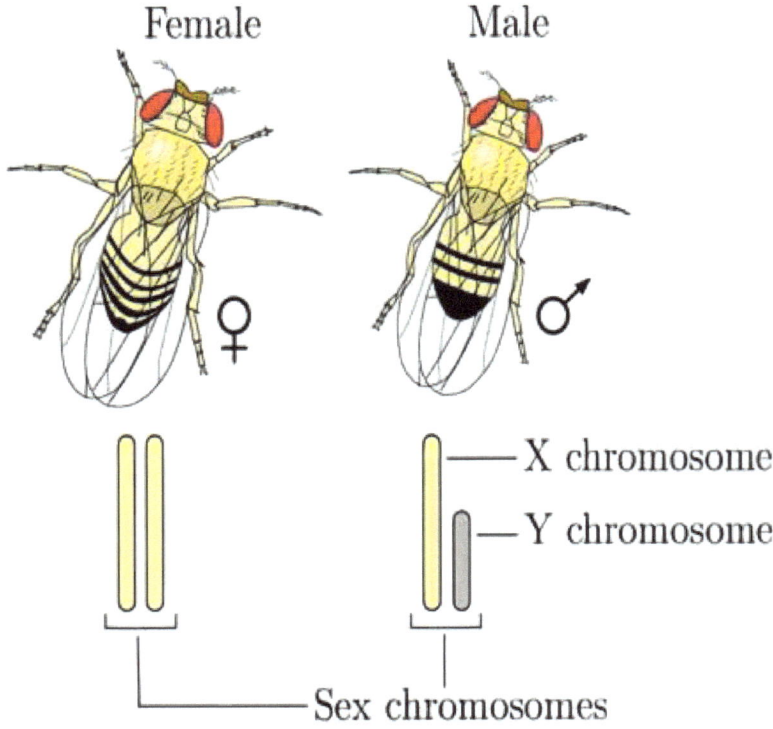

Day 3. I am a little round morula comprised of between 12 and 16 blastomeres.

My size as a morula (1) and blastula (2).

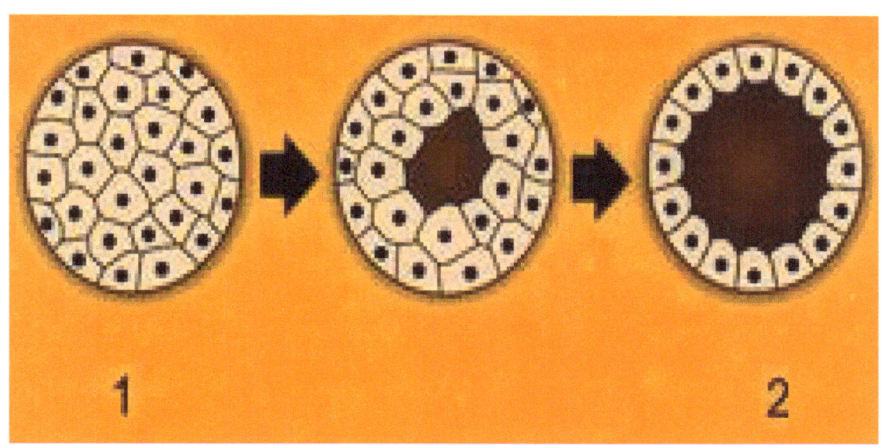

Day 4. I am a free-floating blastocyst and believe it or not, I will attach to my mother's uterus in two days.

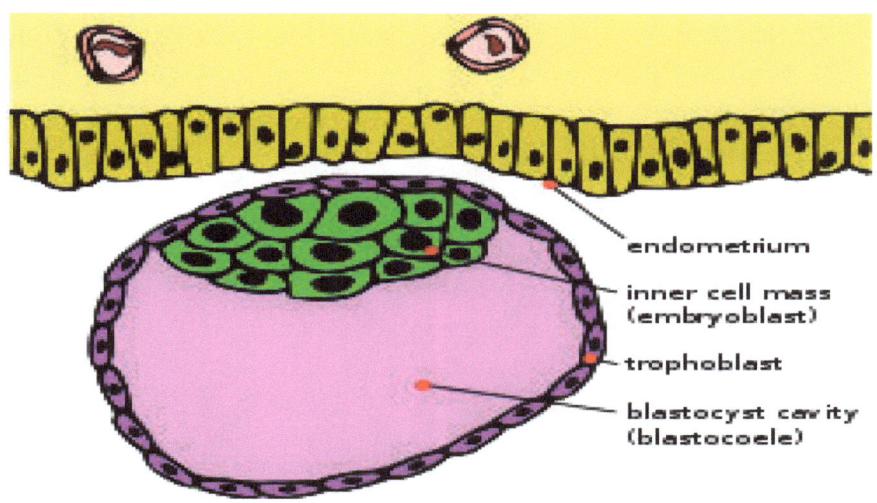

Day 5. I am a hatching blastocyst. It makes me feel like a cute baby chick.

"Zona hatching is a phenomenon occurring during prenatal development. Prior to this event, the predecessor of the embryo, in the form of a blastocyst, is surrounded by a glycoprotein sphere called the zona pellucida. To be able to perform implantation on the uterine wall, the blastocyst first needs to get rid of the zona pellucida. This lysis of the zona pellucida is called the zona hatching."[1]

Is this not the coolest explanation? Do not worry. I will not speak like this for the next 38 weeks. This conversation between me and my grandpa used more scientific words, as he is a doctor, but from here, the language used in this book is simple enough for anyone to understand.

Day 6. Have you heard of the placenta? I feel like an astronaut in a tiny capsule attaching for dear life to my mother's ship.

Day 7. The placenta begins to form. This is where my "capsule" will attach to my mom, and thanks to the umbilical cord, I will get nutrients and oxygen to be able to develop. I promised you no fancy words, so instead, here is a picture to explain for those who are interested.

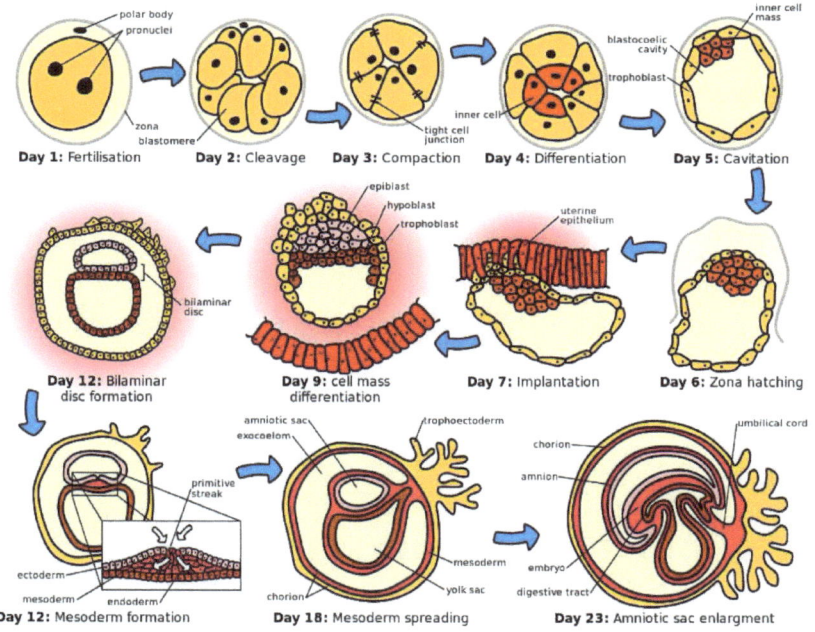

March 17, 2016

Week 1

Day 1. I'll never forget this day. My mom and dad were so happy to get the positive pregnancy test. They couldn't believe it was real, but it was. It was real love; they were going to have another baby! My mom rushed to call Aunt Nono and tell her the good news. I was just as excited and couldn't wait to meet them.

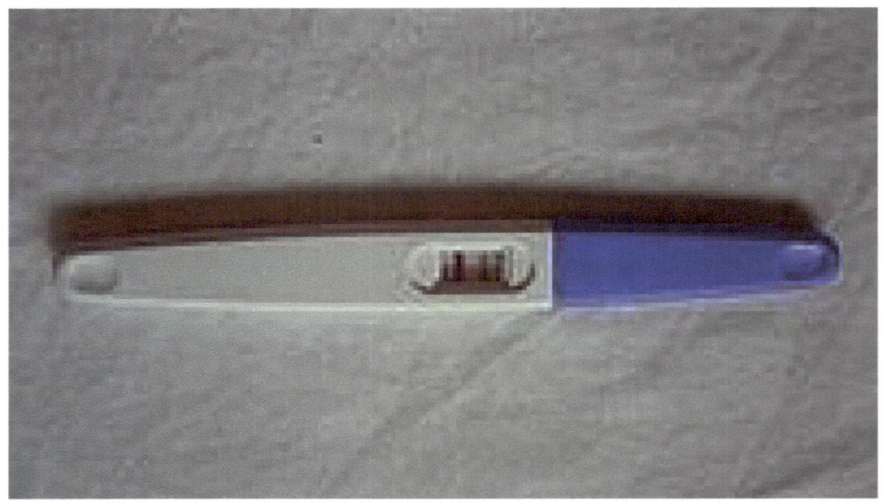

Day 5. My implantation is complete. My parents are stuck with me now! This wonderful, their sweet girl is coming in about 36 weeks to make their life special.

March 24, 2016 (Size: 0.118")

Week 2

I know I am going to be smart because my brain is the first organ to form. I can already comprehend that 2 + 2 = 4.

My intestines are formed and since I am clever, I know that once they are all fully formed, it means I can eat and poop.

I am now the size of a poppy seed that is inside one of these pods. That's pretty tiny, but I won't stay this way for long.

March 31, 2016 (Size: 0.13")

Week 3

I'm in love. I can feel my heart starting to form. My parents will hear it soon, how exciting! I need umbilical arteries and veins, so they are also appearing. And I have no idea what it does, but I have a full thyroid.

I am now the size of a ladybug. I bet I'll be just as cute and loveable. Maybe red will be my favorite color?

April 7, 2016 (Size: 0.25", weight negligible)
Week 4

My lower limb buds are supplied with nerves. Eventually I will practice using them and kick my legs. This is the first touch I will get to share with my mother.

My umbilical cord is emerging...talk about wanting to be attached to my mom! I know she will be very attached to me through this journey and probably forever.

At 4 weeks and 3 days, I start to look like an alien. My eyes have formed on the side of my head, but don't worry, it will get better. I will be beautiful!

I am now 0.25", the size of a *Paedocypris*, the smallest fish found in Indonesia.

April 14, 2016 (Size: 0.4", weight still negligible)
Week 5

This is the time when all my major systems will develop. My four favorites are the cardiovascular, digestive, respiratory, and muscular. I wonder how many of the systems my dad will remember?

I am glad my mom has promised she will not drink during this critical time, because that would be bad for my spinal cord. She already gets points for not being a smoker.

My grandpa told me that when he was in Peru, he had a real hard time saying "pituitary". I laugh because now that I have it, he still cannot say it properly. Ha-ha!

But you know what is really amazing? My heart rhythm is now being configured by specially made pacemaker cells, created just for me.

I am now 0.4", the size of a frog from Papua New Guinea.

April 21, 2016 (Size: 0.5", 0.04oz)
Week 6

Connections are starting to form in my spinal cord; they allow me to feel the information coming from my body. This must be like when my mother tells my brother, "Dear Benjamin, you have to feel your inner self to understand your emotions."

I have teeth buds! In the future, I will be able to chew some great food. When I am born, my parents will be able to see them with my grandpa's great invention, the *Baby Tooth Finder*, even before they erupt.

Also, something interesting: I have nipples along the side of my trunk. I don't know what they are for, but I am very curious to find out.

At 0.5", I am now the size of a Western pygmy blue butterfly from Grand Cayman.

April 28, 2016 (Size: 0.9", 0.07oz)

Week 7

These annoying hiccups...I wish I could control them! It is probably the reason my heart rate has reached 170 beats per minute.

I am now a girl with two ovaries.

Even my heart is growing. It now has four chambers and is almost complete.

I am now 0.9", the size of a petite, colorful guppy fish.

May 5, 2016 (Size: 1.25", 0.14oz)

Week 8

Hey, Mama and Dada, my eardrums are formed this week. You may think it is silly, but go ahead and talk to me, I want to hear your voices. My diaphragm is complete too. I will be able to take real deep breaths before I sing.

At this moment, I already have around 4,000 of the 4,500 body parts that I'll eventually have when I'm an adult.

I am now the size of the smallest known chameleon, and just like it, I will change dresses often. I am sure it will drive my dad nuts.

May 12, 2016 (Size: 1.61", 0.25oz)

Week 9

My face, hands, and feet can sense when someone is touching my mom's belly, so when all her friends touch her belly, I can feel it. I hope the world is gentle with me. If I get anxious, I can always start sucking my thumb.

I still have no idea what the thyroid is, but it keeps growing and now weighs 2 grams. It must be important. I have early reproductive cells in my ovaries, which means one day I can be a mom just as great as my own.

I am now the size of *Papilio machaon*, the larval stage of a very beautiful butterfly.

May 19, 2016 (Size: 2.13", 0.49oz)
Week 10

Now that I know my secondary teeth are budding, I am glad that the tooth fairy will come and collect my primary teeth. If I say *aaaaah,* you can see my palatine tonsils.

My very basic kidney unit called the *glomeruli* has started to form. I wish it formed with a faucet to make it easier to toilet train later on.

I am now the size of a desert hamster and just as cute and cuddly.

May 26, 2016 (Size: 2.9", 0.81oz)

Week 11

My nose and lips are completely formed, and I have started making very complex facial expressions. I wish I had a mirror to see how endearing and funny I will be!

I am now the size of a bee hummingbird, native to Cuba and the Isle of Pines. My parents will know when I am happy because I will be humming my delightful songs.

June 2, 2016 (Size: 3.9", 1.5oz)
Week 12

My mother sneaked some sushi today. I know this because my taste buds are currently fully developed.

My brother will like this one: I can make poops now, but I don't need diapers because it goes straight into the amniotic fluid. Life inside is easy.

That thyroid I told you about is producing something called hormones, and without them, I would have serious developmental issues.

I am now the size of a tiny turtle from Little Namaqualand, South Africa. But trust me, when I run from my brother, I will be as fast as a hare.

June 9, 2016 (Size: 4", 2.4oz)
Week 13

My sense of touch is so much better now. I am really looking forward to touching everything in my new future world, especially being touched and hugged by my family.

I do not cough yet, but I am preparing to do it by growing little hairs called "cilia" within my airways.

I heard the obstetrician say that I am 4 inches from crown to heel.

I am now the size of a sea urchin, but unlike them, I only have one spine.

June 16, 2016 (Size: 4.5", 3.5oz)
Week 14

My grandpa, who is a pediatrician, told my parents that I am a girl because my jaws are moving very fast. Even if this is true, I know that my brother, Benjamin, will always be more of a talker than me.

My crown to heel measurement is now 4.5 inches, and there's that crown talk again! I have a feeling that I will dress up as a princess wearing a crown often.

My cerebellum in my brain is almost like an adult one; it will help me with my muscle tone, equilibrium, and balance. I am glad I have plenty more time to get better at all these functions.

I am now the size of a green anole (*Anolis carolinensis*) from the Carolinas. Sometimes they call it the American chameleon, even if it is not a true chameleon. I hope they didn't name me after this creature!

June 23, 2016 (Size: 5.12", 4.94oz)
Week 15

I am starting to store body fat. My mom is already worrying about me being too chubby. I am not eating any real food yet, however my digestive enzymes are preparing for their future tough task.

I am now the size of a laboratory mouse. I promise I will donate my now-formed stem cells to anybody that needs them to have a better life.

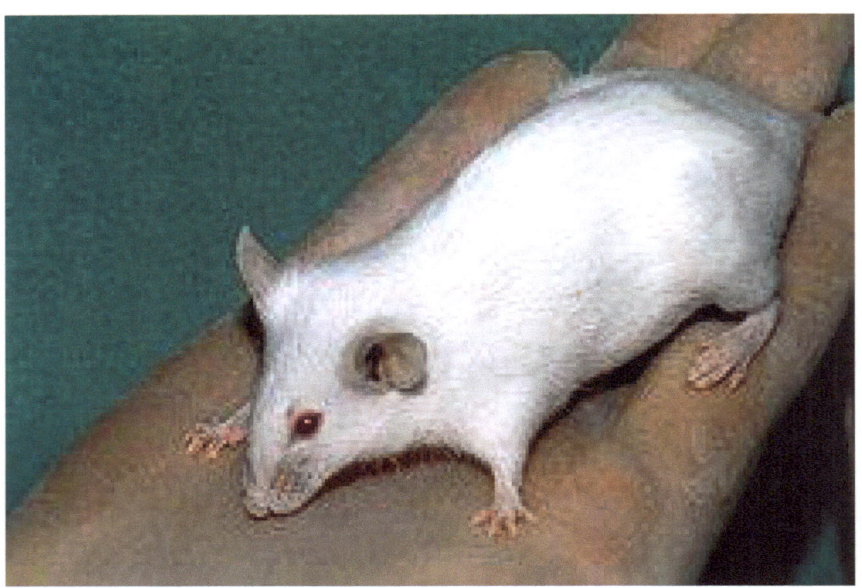

June 30, 2016 (Size: 5.5", 6.7oz)

Week 16

Hey Grandpa, I have news for you! I am 21 centimeters long, my bronchial tree is almost complete, and I have teeth enamel now, so get your *Baby Tooth Finder* ready!

Have you heard of quickening? It is an amusing term for the funny fluttering my mom feels in her tummy when I do my daily exercises.

I am now the size of a red factor canary, that was first bred in 1920.

July 7, 2016 (Size: 6", 8.4oz)

Week 17

My heart has already beat 20 million times, and I am planning to do it trillions more.

I am grateful that my retina has discrete layers at this point, because I am very eager and curious to see what our world looks like.

I am now the size of a desert hedgehog. I'm told my cousins in Israel have seen some.

July 14, 2016 (Size: 10.5", 10oz)
Week 18

I now can practice what kind of cry I will have when I am born. I will make sure it is as high a pitch as possible. I know my dad will love that.

Some people sweat a lot. I am trying to hold off having too many sweat glands, especially under the armpits.

My corpus callosum is complete! This is a fiber bundle of about 300 million fibers in the human brain that connects the two cerebral hemispheres. The interhemispheric functions of the corpus callosum include the integration of perceptual, cognitive, learned, and decision-making information.

I am now the size of a golden lion tamarin, native to the forests of Brazil. If I look like her, will my dad call me "my cute little monkey"?

July 21, 2016 (Size: 10.58", 12oz)
Week 19

My breathing patterns, body movements, and heart rate have started to follow daily cycles in a fancy term called *circadian rhythms*. Will I be a good or bad sleeper? I wonder if that will be determined early in my life?

I am trying to collect as much melanin as I can because my mom always worries that Benjamin and I are going to get burned outside if it is sunny. Personally, I want to see the sun and warm myself.

I am now the size of a Roman Ladies' Dog from the island of Malta in the Mediterranean. She looks as fair as my mom's skin.

July 28, 2016 (Size: 11", 15oz)

Week 20

My mom is a speech therapist and is less nervous about my speech development because I can hear now. When she sings in the shower, I can finally hear her beautiful voice!

I weigh a whole pound now, and my length from crown to heel is 11 inches.

I am now the size of a Yorkshire terrier. This beauty is one of the yappiest dogs in the world. I can't wait for the day I get to talk to my mom and dad!

August 4, 2016 (Size: 11.4", 1.1lbs)
Week 21

Want to know something amazing? If I was born today, I would have a high chance of survival. But don't worry Mom, it is very comfortable in here, so if you guys don't mind, I am staying inside for much longer.

You know what else is amazing? My heartbeat is loud enough that my grandpa can listen to it with his stethoscope. He says my heart is strong. That's because it's already so full of love for my family.

I have a favorite position to sleep in; it is very close to my mom's heart. I try not to bother her, especially at night, because I know it makes her burp a lot.

I am now the size of a Mauritius fruit bat, which reminds me of how often I am upside down, and my parents don't even know it. A preface to a great gymnast!

August 11, 2016 (Size:12", 1.3lbs)
Week 22

My heart has now beat 30 million times. I heard my parents talking about something called mega millions. They want to win it to move some place bigger, but I feel like an astronaut floating around in space. I like my home.

My eyelids may be shut but my eyeballs are moving, and I have little white fuzzies on my eyebrows. I can't wait to put make up on them. Of course, I know that won't be for many years.

I am now the size of a Californian brush rabbit, which is a species of cottontail rabbit and is soft, like me.

August 18, 2016 (Size: 13.6", 1.5lbs)
Week 23

I have achieved breathing motions up to 44 times per minute. I am practicing because I know my parents will want me to dive into my grandparent's pool very soon after birth.

My brain weighs 100 grams, a little over 3 oz. I am so smart!

I am now the size of this funny looking blobfish. I will definitely not look like this, but of course I will be funny. My brother and I will be a pair of comedians and my mom and dad will rejoice with our humorous family.

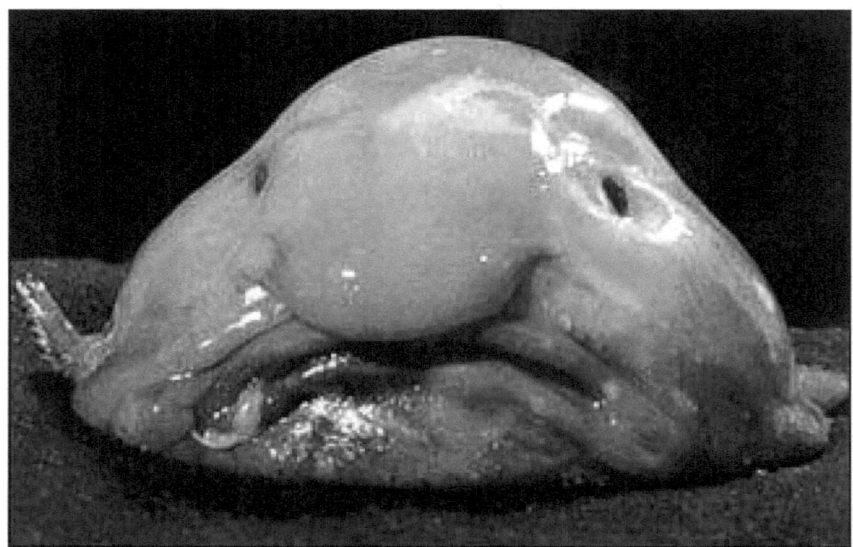

August 25, 2016 (Size: 14", 1.7lbs)
Week 24

My family has started a bet over if I will be a boy or girl, how long I will be, and how much I will weigh. I wish I could tell my parents I am a girl, because of course I want them to win.

Right now, the doctors say I am about 1.7 pounds and 14 inches long.

I am now the size of a squirrel and just as agile, despite how tight it is getting in my mom's belly.

September 1, 2016 (Size: 14.4", 1.9lbs)
Week 25

My thigh bones are about two inches long: chunky, chunky!

I am now the size of a blueface angelfish. It is one of the most beautiful fish in the Indo-Pacific Ocean. My mom will be surprised by how quickly I learn to swim, but I will play it safe like an angel.

September 8, 2016 (My size: 15", 2.2lbs)
Week 26

I can produce tears now, which will be much needed to get my parents on my side when my brother is roughhousing with me. Also, I know my dad is a farter because he can stimulate my sense of smell.

I am now the size of the viscacha, a rodent from Peru and Chile. To honor my Peruvian relatives, I chose this animal to compare my size. Hopefully, when I visit them, I will get to see one!

September 15, 2016 (Size:15.2", 2.5lbs)
Week 27

Even though it is really dark in here, my pupils react to the world's light.

I am now the size of a blind fish, which is native to Mexico.

September 22, 2016 (Size: 15.7", 2.91lbs)
Week 28

I can now distinguish sounds at different frequencies. I love the deep sound of my father's voice. My mother has a musical voice, and that makes me want to kick my feet. Maybe I'll be a dancer? I am not sure what to think of my brother's shrieks when it is his bedtime though.

I am now the size of a toucan found in Latin American countries. What a colorful animal! I hope I can see it when I visit my great grandmother, Eva, in Peru.

September 29, 2016 (Size: 16.2", 3lbs)
Week 29

I can regulate my own temperature now, but I prefer my mother's cozy environment.

I am now the size of a Mandarin duck found in East Asia. They tend to be shy and seek cover under hanging willow trees. I wonder if I will become shy at times and want to hide under my grandparent's big willow tree?

October 6, 2016 (Size: 16.7", 3.8lbs)
Week 30

My head is now close to 10 inches of all-girl brain power that will allow me to participate in the national geography bee!

With my nails now fully developed, I dream of painting my toenails and fingernails pink. No, blue. Wait! Maybe green… I am relieved I have a few more weeks to decide!

I am now the size of a Cape hare native to Africa and Arabia. I kick my legs lots as I try to run. I will probably run so fast that one day I will be the captain of the running team in high school.

October 13, 2016 (Size: 17.2", 4.2lbs)
Week 31

I don't know why most information at this stage states I am the size of a pineapple. Maybe my mom is having a virgin piña colada!?

The picture below is not my size and is not even an animal. I just couldn't resist showing my mom what I know she is missing. Meanwhile, my dad sips his as they wonder what I will be like when I grow up.

October 20, 2016 (Size: 17.7", 4.7lbs)
Week 32

I am starting to remember things in the musical word. My mother sings so beautifully that she was considering entering a contest called *American Idol*. I know she would have won. I love being in my dad's car when he plays classical music. It is soothing to my brother, Benjamin.

I am now the size of an American Mink (*Neovison vison*). I am semiaquatic and native to the USA.

October 27, 2016 (Size: 18", 5.3lbs)
Week 33

I am now acquiring taste preferences. So far, I like chicken and broccoli the best.

I am now the size of an 18-inch platter of sushi. I wish my mom would eat sushi again. I would love to try it.

November 3, 2016 (Size: 18.6", 5.78lbs)
Week 34

Ouch! I am rapidly gaining weight. In the past week I gained 7.68 ounces. My mom worries that gaining too much weight will be unhealthy for both of us. She already cares so much for me. I love you, Mom.

I don't know what my size compares to now, but I hope I don't look like this cat!

November 10, 2016 (Size: 19", 6.3lbs)
Week 35

Hey, Mom and Dad, you should feel my strength! I have a solid grip. And though I will share toys with my brother, sometimes I may be assertive and not let go.

I am now the size of a rusty-spotted cat. It is one of the cat family's smallest members. Look at those eyes! I think mine will be blue and softly piercing.

November 17, 2016 (Size: 19.5", 6.8lbs)
Week 36

My brain is now 10 ounces, and I am considered full term. Everybody thinks I am comfy in here and that I don't want to come out. That's not true. I am curious what my new world will be like, but it seems my mom is not ready yet.

I am now the size of this marten. I will soon weasel my way out and say hello to everybody reading this book. Pun intended!

November 24, 2016 (Size: 20", 7lbs)
Week 37

My mom has gone to the hospital a few times, but the poor thing was sent home and told to wait longer. I feel her contractions that have a name that sounds like a motorcycle's name, "Braxton Hicks".

I can drink 15 oz. of amniotic fluid a day. I heard that my mother is looking forward to breastfeeding me, and I would rather have that.

I could now be the size of a lion cub. My mom's doctor jokes that I am the size of a pumpkin, but I hope my parents don't call me their "little pumpkin". I am just me, sweet Caroline Eva.

December 1, 2016 (Size: 10.2", 7.6lbs)

Week 38

I am finally born at 5:22 a.m. I am 24 inches long, and my weight is 9 pounds and 8 ounces. I am long and chunky! Ha! Nobody won the bet about my birth measurements.

I can see. I can touch. I can smell. I can hear and right away I start eating. Oh, wow! Life is so wonderful outside that I cry for joy! I hope my parents understand this and don't think that I am crying because I am tired, cranky, hungry, gassy, teething, wet, hot, or cold.

I am so happy to be part of this world. I will be sweet. I will give joy. I will be the best sister to my brother Benjamin. I will love my bath. I will fall asleep in two seconds. I will toilet train early without fussing. I will eat all the food they give me. I will be the best preschooler there is.

But after that, I cannot promise anything.

Before I finish this journey, let me tell you one last thing: This will be my height when I am 18 years old! And just like a panda, I will be sweet and cuddly!

With abundant love,
Caroline Eva

Disclaimers

Grandpa and I did not discuss political opinions related to my conception or journey.

All the pictures included in this book came from Wikipedia.

1: "Zona Hatching" (Wikipedia, Retrieved 3/8/19
https://en.wikipedia.org/wiki/Zona_hatching.)

Even though my grandpa is a retired pediatrician and researched many websites to be accurate, he learned that there are discrepancies between many baby websites on the internet, scientific or not, so he described my journey with some poetic freedom. Nevertheless, I feel that I am unique.

Thank you, Aunt Nono, you were the greatest editor that my grandpa could find. And finally, to all the members of the Lewitus family, thank you for supporting Grandpa in the incredible journey to deliver this book.

Ricardo Lewitus MD
www.palotec.com
Copyright 2021

www.ingramcontent.com/pod-product-compliance
Lightning Source LLC
Chambersburg PA
CBHW041812040426
42450CB00001B/14